Suzanne's Kashmir
A Magical Journey

Including Essential Travel Infomation

Suzanne's Kashmir
A Magical Journey

Including Essential Travel Infomation

Suzanne Hogsett

Travel Easy Publishing

Text and photos copyright © 2021
by Suzanne Hogsett

All rights reserved. No part of this book may be reproduced, or stored in a retrieval system, or transmitted in any form or by any means, electronic, mechanical, photocopying, recording, or otherwise, without express written permission of the publisher.

ISBN 978-1-879265-13-4
ISBN 1-879265-13-3

Library of Congress Control Number: 2021900180

Travel Easy Publishing
67782 E. Palm Canyon Drive
Suite B104-130
Cathedral City, CA 92234
suzannehogsett@gmail.com
suzannetravels.com

"I don't regret anything I've ever done in life, any choice that I've made. But I'm consumed with regret for the things I didn't do, the choices I didn't make, the things I didn't say. We spend so much time being afraid of failure, afraid of rejection. But regret is the thing we should fear most. Failure is an answer. Rejection is an answer. Regret is an eternal question you will never have an answer to. 'What if . . .' 'If only . . .' 'I wonder what would have . . .' You will never, never know, and it will haunt you for the rest of your days."

Trevor Noah
Born a Crime

Shikaras on Dal Lake

Shops along Dal Lake

Contents

Introduction 1
Maps of India and Kashmir 3
Places visited in Kashmir 4
A window of opportunity 5
The dream begins 11
Surprises 13
Our houseboat 15
A dreamy ride on the lake 21
The surprises of Srinagar 25
Amazing Mughal architecture 33
A day trip to Pahalgam 39
A journey to Sonamarg 45
Our final day: still more to see 55
Final thoughts 63
Afterword 65
Essential travel information 69
   A note about Covid-19 69
   Resources 69
      Tour operator 69
      Travel insurance 70
      Books and magazines 70
      Newspapers printed in English 71
      Online resources 71
      Government advisories 71
   Safety and security 73
   When to go 75
   Getting a visa 76
   Kashmiri culture, beliefs, traditions, and
      practices 78
   Kashmiri food, food safety, and recipes 83
      Kashmiri tea (Kahwa) 84
      Kasmiri lamb curry (Rogan Josh) 85

Chicken Yakhni	87
Banana fritters with raisins and powdered sugar	88
How to dress	89
What to bring–a packing list for Kashmir and all of India	90
Luggage	90
Documents	91
Electronics/electrical	91
Clothing	92
Security	93
Shoes	93
Laundry	93
Eyeglasses	94
Medicines/first aid	94
Toiletries	95
Office supplies	96
Food	96
Food utensils	97
Miscellaneous	97
What to shop for and how to bargain	98
Key buys in Kashmir	98
The art of bargaining	99
Dealing with money	102
How to get around	104
About the author	105
A note from the author	111

Introduction

We all have dreams, or at least we should. Some are short-lived, but the best are life long. While other women may dream of happy homes filled with the joyous laughter of children, that was not my dream. My dreams were travel dreams.

I have always been a renegade, defying custom and tradition, and yearning to escape the mundane, the ordinary, the accepted, the "normal." I fled a traditional middle-class suburban upbringing and, as soon as possible, at age fifteen, I was already off on my first travel adventure. Over time I would travel to some 115 countries and all 50 states. I always cherished my freedom, and for a long time I chose it over the seeming security of a steady job, owning a house, having a husband. I strove to know the world as a traveler, as an adventurer, as a participant, and never, never ever, as a mere sightseer, as just a tourist. I embarked with will and determination on the road less traveled, and at times on no road at all; just a path perhaps, at best. I chose most often to travel alone, with only my camera in hand as a steady and trusted companion.

Yet, in all my years of wandering the globe, one dream remained. It had always been my favorite dream, my dream of dreams. Yet it was the dream that always eluded me. My dream was to visit and come to know Kashmir, the part administered by India, in India's far north. I'd made so many lengthy, far reaching trips to almost every part of India, but in all those years traveling safely to often politically volatile Kashmir had rarely seemed possible.

In 1947, when the British Raj finally collapsed and British rule of India ended, the independent countries of India and Pakistan were born. What to do about the region of predominantly Muslim Kashmir became a dilemma. Should a Muslim state belong to Muslim Pakistan, or to adjoining Hindu India?

The governing Maharaja of Kashmir had the voice that mattered, and his choice was for Kashmir to join India. India and Pakistan both immediately sent in troops, and a cease-fire two years later resulted in Kashmir being partitioned between the two countries. An unofficial border, the tenuous United Nations demarcated "Line of Control" was created, which is still in effect. All of Kashmir is still claimed by both countries, and a very small part is even claimed by China. Since partition there have been numerous incursions, border wars, and some grizzly incidents, yet even these were followed by periods of peace.

For decades these incidents thwarted even the idea of me planning a trip to Kashmir. But it haunted me. I'd never stopped dreaming about going. I'd always longed to stay on a traditional houseboat, take gondola-like boats along placid Dal Lake, explore the canals, see alpine-like scenery and glaciers up close, ride horses, taste unique dishes, shop for Kashmir's famous intricately designed handicrafts, walk in centuries-old gardens with waterfalls, and learn more about Muslim traditions and culture.

This seemingly hidden corner of the world awaited, as if wanting to reveal itself to me, almost as if it were magic. It all seemed to be something so enchanting, so mysterious, and so special that I had to make it happen. It "called" to me, and in 2019 I knew that I could no longer ignore the quest. Somehow I would make it happen. Nothing would stop me. I was going.

Maps of India and Kashmir

Kashmir is located in India's far north

Places visited in Kashmir

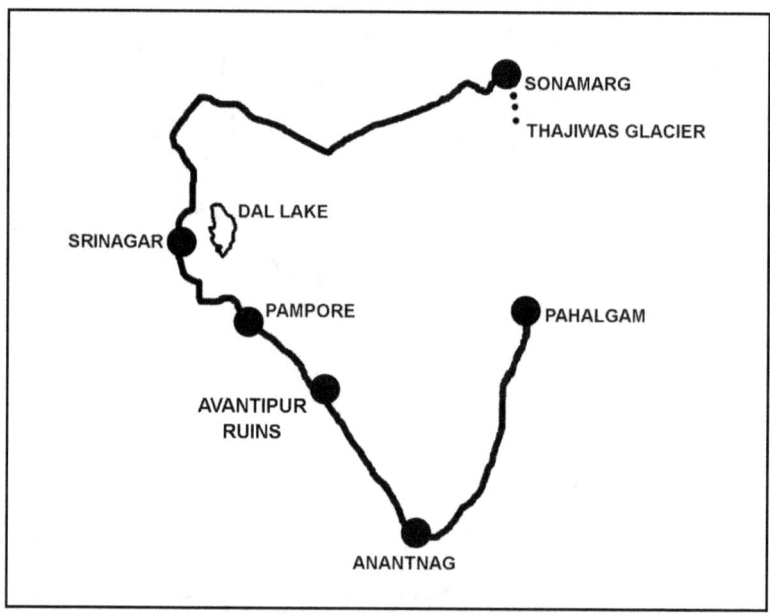

A window of opportunity

In early 2019, as there seemed to be a long-lasting lull in the many problematic political incidents, I saw a window of opportunity. I hurriedly booked a tour of Kashmir and Ladakh with an American tour company located near San Francisco. It promised to be a cultural and educational tour, and there would be seven other tour members, all of whom were well traveled. We would see only the part of Kashmir administered by India, not the part under Pakistani control. The trip was to start in mid-September. I redeemed some frequent flier miles for an airline ticket to India, and my suitcase was soon packed. I counted the days, anxiously waiting. I was ready to go.

But on August 5 Indian Prime Minister Modi's primarily Hindu government removed Article 370 of the Indian constitution. This article had long guaranteed a fair degree of autonomy to the state of Jammu and Kashmir. It had its own flag, its own constitution, and the right to make its own laws. Under the 1973 Delhi agreement Kashmiris became full Indian citizens, and the central government in Delhi couldn't send in troops without Kashmiri government agreement. The Indian government only had influence over citizenship, supreme court rulings, foreign affairs, communications and defense.

Prime Minister Modi had kept his recent election promise to his predominantly Hindu constituents: India's central government would repeal Article 370 of its constitution. He'd won the election by a landslide, and he now felt empowered to act.

So on August 5 Hindu pilgrims, migrant workers and many thousands of tourists enjoying their summer holidays in the region were told to leave immediately. Jammu and Kashmir was no longer a state. It had become a "federally administered region," now called a "Union Territory." The local legislature was suspended. Prominent Kashmiri leaders, including the chief minister, were arrested, and there were warnings that anyone opposing Modi's move would be jailed as well. The collapse of tourism, which had long been the region's biggest income source, shattered the local economy.

Fearing retaliation by the Kashmiris, the Indian government increased its military presence to some reported 600,000 soldiers, barred all tourism, cut off almost all phone and internet services in the region, and imposed a curfew.

Realizing that my long hoped for and long awaited journey would now suddenly be dead in the water, I awaited the dreaded call from the tour company. I'd just hoped that the phone wouldn't ring, and I was relieved at the end of each day when no call came. Then my luck ran out. The tour company had no choice but to cancel the Kashmir portion of the trip, as tourists had been banned from Kashmir, and it looked like the situation wasn't going to change any time soon. What else could the company do?

The Ladakh portion of the trip was still a go however, so in early September I forged ahead and flew to Ladakh, just east of Kashmir, where, along with seven other tour members, I was steeped in Buddhist culture at one monastery after the other. After the tour ended I headed to other parts of India: Goa, Sikkim, Darjeeling and Rishikesh.

While in India I monitored the political and security situation in Kashmir closely, on a daily basis. I read the *Times of India* and other Indian newspapers, talked to tour guides, checked the internet, and watched English-speaking news channels on television. I kept hoping that Kashmir would remain calm enough for the Indian government to reopen the region to tourism before I had to leave India in early

November. And, if they opened it up, I hoped it would be safe to go.

On October 8, as my time in India had started to run out, I was overjoyed to learn that tourists were now allowed to visit Kashmir again. Luckily it had remained peaceful, with very few problematic incidents. On October 21, having just completed a Sikkim and Darjeeling itinerary that I'd already committed to, I called the New Delhi tour company, The Travel Circuit, which had booked the Sikkim trip for me. I asked if they thought that travel to Kashmir would be safe and, if so, if they could quickly book an itinerary for me. They assured me that it was safe, and after an excellent experience in Sikkim with them, I felt confident that I could trust their word.

Although I often traveled the world alone, and my husband hadn't signed up for the original Kashmir and Ladakh tour, he now wanted to see Kashmir. So he joined me. The Travel Circuit quickly proposed an itinerary for October 24–28. It included round-trip airfare for the two of us from New Delhi to Srinagar, Kashmir, four nights on a deluxe houseboat moored on Dal Lake in Srinagar, all breakfasts and dinners on board, rides in a small gondola-like boat from the town's jetty to the houseboat and back, an English-speaking local guide and a driver, an air-conditioned Toyota Innova car for four days, all sightseeing and entrance fees in town and on day trips to the countryside, airport arrival and departure transfers, and all taxes. We paid the equivalent of $960 for the two of us plus a 3.5% credit card fee, for a total of $994. To get a better exchange rate we paid in Indian rupees rather than in US dollars. Yet having paid so little for what seemed to be so much, I wondered if it were all just too good to be true. Would I be bitterly disappointed? Would my lifelong dream just turn out to have been a fantasy, an illusion not grounded in reality, and nothing more?

As there were then just three days before the trip would start, we flew to New Delhi to quickly prepare. A Travel Circuit representative met us at our lodging to hand us our e-tickets for the flights, a detailed itinerary, and phone numbers for our driver and guide. He imprinted our credit card for payment, and answered the questions we had.

I quickly perused all the voluminous bookstores in New Delhi for books on Kashmir. There were quite a few, but all focused solely on Kashmir's history, its wars, its turmoil. None focused on the beauty of this special place or offered any insights into what to see and do. I then vowed to change that and to commit to doing just that after my visit. And so the idea of writing this book was born.

As no one seemed to know if any ATMs would be working in Kashmir, I used my no-fee Charles Schwab bank debit card at a number of ATMs in Delhi in order to get the equivalent of US $800 in Indian rupees. This would cover the costs of any non-included meals, tips, and shopping. Because the ATMs we used limited transactions to 10,000 rupees each, ($142), it took six transactions to get the needed cash.

We'd also brought money belts, worn around our waists under our clothes, and long pants and long-sleeved shirts, so we could dress modestly, in keeping with Muslim mores. Before leaving for India we'd also purchased travel insurance, including emergency medical evacuation, and we'd registered with the US State Department's STEP, the Smart Traveler Enrollment Program. STEP would notify us in case of any emergency in the areas we were set to travel in. Before leaving home we'd also stocked up on snacks such as almonds, Kind bars, herbal teas, dried apricots, Stevia, Pita Bite crackers, Wheat Thins, Pepperidge Farm Goldfish and instant noodle soups, for what might turn out to be long day trips and for any emergency meals.

The dream begins

On October 24, before heading to the airport in New Delhi for a lunchtime flight to Srinagar on SpiceJet, one of several daily flights from Delhi, other points in India and Dubai, I checked the internet, international news channels on television, and *Times of India* for any critical last-minute information about security in Kashmir. Thankfully I saw nothing to be concerned about. As the Indian government's shutdown of almost all phone and internet services in Kashmir hadn't yet been lifted, we told our friends where we were headed and not to worry if they didn't hear from us for five days.

Expecting an even more lengthy and detailed security screening than usual at the airport, we arrived three hours before the flight. As with all departing flights in India, we needed to show our e-tickets, either as a printout or on our phones, at the entrance to the terminal building before we could enter. To our surprise, there was no extra security screening whatsoever. We then wondered if the security problems in Kashmir that the media had so often reported had been blown out of proportion. Had the Indian and international media exaggerated the risks? I'd seen it happen before in so many places. Was this just another one?

For an hour and a half we flew the 544 miles northwest to Srinagar, Jammu and Kashmir's capital. During the flight we saw up close the impressive snow-capped Himalayas and, just before landing, as we approached the 87-mile long Kashmir Valley, we could see tin-roofed villages, a patchwork of orchards and open fields, and no high-rise buildings. When we landed, another surprise. Everything at the airport seemed calm. There wasn't even a hint of anything out of the ordinary. We, and all foreigners, had to fill out an arrival form. Among other things, it asked for the name of our houseboat. We didn't know it, but fortunately our guide, Majid, had been allowed inside the arrival hall and he gave us the name. It all took less than ten minutes. We quickly retrieved our wheeled bags from the small luggage conveyor belt and we were ready to explore Kashmir.

Surprises

Then there was another surprise: As we walked out to the airport parking lot we saw, along the edge of the runway, so many Indian soldiers in camouflage, all armed with rifles, and several pillbox bunkers. We met our driver, Mehraj, hopped into our roomy Toyota Innova car, and drove the 10 miles to Dal Lake. We noticed how clean the streets were, totally devoid of trash. There were no cows in the middle of the road, no garbage dumped nearby, few people, quiet streets, and very little traffic. We already felt very far removed from the India we had just left a few hours before.

Srinagar's unpolluted and serene setting, ringed by the green Pir Panjal mountains, has as its jewels placid Dal and Nagin Lakes. The city and the surrounding Kashmir Valley have long been idyllic summer retreats for emperors of antiquity, as well as more recently for well-to-do Indians, and British and other foreign tourists. The mile high elevation and moderate climate, with October temperatures in the 70s, made us decide to spend most of our time outdoors.

We stopped for lunch near Dal Lake at Stream restaurant, which offered a variety of Indian dishes. We ordered the rogan josh, a lamb dish and speciality of Kashmir made with yogurt and a spicy red Kashmiri chili sauce, and rice, and paid the US equivalent of $5.40 for the two of us. But when we tried the dish there was barely any meat, just bones. Unable to find our guide and driver to ask for help, we just ate the sauce with the rice, which was still quite tasty. Then we learned that traditionally the guide and driver always ate separately from their passengers. We were also told that, following Muslim tradition, Kashmir was a "dry state," meaning no alcohol was served in restaurants or elsewhere. So no beer for lunch! We later called Stream Restaurant "The Bones Restaurant," and we just hoped that other meals would be better.

After a short drive we arrived at a lakeside jetty and met Gulhar, our private shikara man, who would ferry us from the jetty to our houseboat and back for our five-day stay on the lake. Shikaras are colorful gondola-like water taxis which seat six, have canopied roofs and curtains, and often have large comfy cushions covered in flowered pattern fabrics. They are navigated by a rower at one end of the boat, who rows with a single large heart-shaped paddle. Non-motorized, they are perfectly quiet, and are open-aired, so we could see plenty of scenery as we glided by.

Shikaras are similar to gondolas

Mahjong was moored on Dal Lake

Our houseboat

Gulhar rowed us for a fifteen-minute scenic ride through picturesque narrow canals on spring-fed Dal Lake before arriving at our houseboat, named Mahjong.

Our houseboat Mahjong

We passed houseboats with names like Hilton Kashmir (no relation), Cherryripe, Mumtaz Palace and Shabistan. We thought it odd that someone would name their houseboat Shabistan. Was it really shabby? But then we learned that a shabistan is a covered part of a mosque.

Of the roughly twelve hundred houseboats said to be moored on Dal and Nagin Lakes and along the Jhelum River in town, it looked like very few were occupied, as tourists had not yet returned.

When we arrived and stepped aboard Mahjong we were warmly welcomed by Ahmad, our houseboat man, who would serve as both our host and waiter. He was a gentle soft-spoken older Muslim man who spoke perfect English. He told us he'd been working on the boat since he was twelve years old.

Our houseboat man Ahmad on the verandah

The houseboats are often elaborate single story large long, narrow barge-like vessels crafted out of cedar wood. Unlike those in Kerala, these are often more sumptuous, and these don't move. They are moored in large rows and are tightly packed in, with the boat next door sitting just a few yards away from ours.

During the Raj era, from 1858 to 1947, when the British ruled India, Britons who lived in India came in droves to Kashmir's lakes for summer holidays, as a reprieve from India's torrid summer temperatures further south.

At the time foreigners weren't allowed to own land or anything on it anywhere in India, so they built houseboats as a ruse in order to evade the law. And it worked. Because the boats weren't on land, they didn't count as property. Many of today's houseboats are originals, built in the colonial era, while many newer ones are still inspired by the same tradition.

The boats come in five categories: Deluxe, A, B, C, and D, are of various sizes, and most are family run. The interiors of the deluxe boats like ours are opulent. The sitting rooms, dining rooms and bedrooms are fitted out with glitzy over-the-top chandeliers, faceted wood ceilings and paneling, heavily embroidered crewel curtains, carved walnut furniture, and Kashmiri carpets with intricate designs. Our sitting room, which could seat about twenty people, looked like a Victorian parlor and was very comfortable. The only clue that we lived in a modern age was the working television, which carried a number of high quality English-speaking news stations like the BBC and Al Jazeera.

Mahjong's elegant sitting room

The houseboat was spotlessly clean, came with an always smiling and accommodating cook, a refrigerator for our use, and a large verandah in front with cushioned benches. There was a small galley kitchen prep area, but no larger kitchen, as food was prepared in a kitchen on land just behind the boat and brought in at meal times.

As no other travelers were staying on the boat, we were offered a choice of the four en-suite decked out bedrooms. The back bedroom was the largest and most opulent, had twin beds, and was superbly decorated, but we chose a smaller one with a large king bed. (You can bring your own group and have the boat all to yourselves, or you can just occupy one room and possibly share the common areas with other travelers.)

Our bedroom had a carved wood canopy bed, half a dozen pillows, sculpted wood ceiling and wall panels, carved wood tables and desk, embroidered crewel curtains, an embroidered floral bedspread, big bath towels, and a wall heater which went on at night. All rooms came with inelegant but functional Western-style bathrooms, replete with a bathtub/shower and ample hot water.

Our bedroom on Mahjong

Although Ahmad was always there to watch over the boat, we always locked our room and took our passports with us when we left, as access to the boat by outsiders appeared fairly easy. When Ahmad wasn't in the front sitting room the boat's two wooden entrance doors slid together and could be locked however.

Ahmad offered us endless cups of hot Kashmiri tea, called *kahwa*, made with green tea and flavored with cinnamon, saffron and cardamom. It smelled and tasted divine. We then relaxed on the verandah in the sunny warm weather, where we read books and enjoyed views of the lake and the mountains.

This day, and toward the end of every day, we got a call from the tour company in New Delhi asking how things were going. I wondered, given the government's shutdown of phone service, how they'd managed to get through. In any case, although we never had any major concerns to report, it was certainly reassuring that the company was checking in.

Our bathroom on Mahjong

A dreamy ride on the lake

In late afternoon, just an hour before sunset, Gulhar, our shikara man, took us for a leisurely ride on four-mile-long, two-and-one-half-mile-wide Dal Lake. Amidst thick foliage in the water we saw vast clusters of budding yellow water lilies and lotus, a gaggle of about a dozen white geese, and quacking red and yellow beaked ducks with black heads.

Our Shakira ride on Dal Lake

We glided past vast agricultural fields, old houses and shops on stilts, floating gardens made from bulrushes, canoes bearing flowers, small old wooden bridges that seemed to wobble as locals walked over them, and people just quietly going about their daily lives on the water. No noisy motorized boats disrupted the calm. Some areas seemed clogged with lotus blossoms, but other areas had been cleared enough for small boat traffic to pass through. Men and women in wooden boats weeded lotus plants with wooden poles.

Of the hundreds of houseboats we passed, only a handful seemed occupied and it looked like Kashmiri families rather than tourists were living in them.

We returned from our fascinating tour of the lake to a dinner served on a massive ornately carved wood table with eight high-backed chairs. There was a splendid silver tea service in a corner cabinet that looked like it might have been there since the Raj.

Mahjong's elegant dining room

We always had a choice of meal times and an almost unlimited selection of what we wanted to eat. We could choose vegetarian or non-vegetarian food and could ask for any special dishes that appealed to us. Although we usually ate only vegetarian food in India, we made an exception here due to Kashmir's reputation for their chicken, lamb and mutton specialties. Everything was spotlessly clean and all the main dishes were well cooked and served piping hot. Along with several fresh vegetable dishes and banana fritters with raisins and powdered sugar on top, we had a delicious chicken dish, chicken yakhni, made with yogurt, onions, cinnamon, cardamom, and cumin. We asked to have our food made without a lot of chilies.

Dinner aboard Mahjong

Unlike our experiences in other parts of India, where the food was often so spicy that we couldn't eat it, in Kashmir there was never a problem. Everything was yummy, but since at each meal there was more food than we could eat, we stored the rest in the refrigerator to reheat for a meal the next night.

Locally made cookies and fresh fruit were also left out for us in the dining room for snacking. Somehow someone managed to buy some large bottles of Kingfisher Indian beer for us at about three dollars a bottle, which we stowed in the refrigerator. Safe filtered drinking water and tea were included at all meals in the dining room. There were also pitchers of it in the bedroom, and large sealed water bottles were also always there for us in the car.

After dinner, another surprise! Colorful shikara-riding merchants, whose shikaras had become floating shops, came on board unannounced to display before us all sorts of local goods, ranging from Pashmina shawls to large papier-mâché vases, all in our sitting room. While we listened attentively and admired the quality of what we were shown, it was too early in our trip and too late in the day for shopping. Ahmad told the men we weren't interested and they gently went on their way.

Shop along the canal

The surprises of Srinagar

After a sound sleep we awoke to the smell of freshly brewed Kashmiri spice tea. My husband was served hot water to which he added packets of instant Starbucks coffee which he'd brought from home.

Along with the drinks came generous helpings of locally made breads, *tsot* and *tsochvoru*, made with sesame and poppy seeds. There was also fresh fruit and tasty cheese omelets.

As we left Mahjong for our full day trip to explore the city, we rode in our shikara through narrow canals toward the jetty to meet our car and driver. We passed dozens of small shops close to our houseboat in the Nehru Park area, all raised on wooden stilts to just above the water line.

There were quite a few grocers, each with small shops jam packed with hundreds of products. We could see large bags of rice, soap, shampoo, teas, lots of soft drinks, fruit juices, bottled water, cookies, ice cream, and the almost universally available Kit Kat bars.

Some shopkeepers sat outside their shops, awaiting customers that they hoped would soon come. But we saw few customers. We saw nothing fresh, as fruits and vegetables were bought in outdoor markets elsewhere in the city, and from vendors with small boats filled with them. A number of small shops boasted that they were "factory showrooms."

A Muslim shopkeeper awaits customers

A local pharmacy

There were also quite a few pharmacies, called chemists, in the English tradition, and numerous handicraft shops. These too seemed to pack hundreds, if not thousands, of items into very small spaces that at times couldn't have been more than three yards wide. Others looked like they'd been there for a century or more, with doors made from homemade wooden planks nailed together, and with locking padlocks.

The two story post office sat on stilts at the edge of the lake and was something we'd never seen before. It could be accessed by boat on one side and from the street on the other.

The Nehru Park floating post office

A wide array of narrow wooden boats hauled goods, and many colorful shikaras and houseboats could be seen far and wide. Some boats carried products for tourists, such as pretty fabric outfits, which seemed to be good quality. When the rowers approached us and Gulhar told them we weren't interested, they quietly rowed away. We enjoyed seeing local life along the clear, unpolluted waterway and couldn't believe our good luck in finding a place at times as charming, at times as romantic, as Venice, but without crowds and at just a small fraction of the cost.

So far, what had been promised and what I had hoped for hadn't turned out to be too good to be true after all! No wonder so many Indian couples chose to honeymoon here.

When we reached the jetty our guide Majid told us that there was a *bandh*, a general strike and shutdown. It was a

SUZANNE'S KASHMIR

Muslim Kashmiri protest against the primarily Hindu Indian government's reneging on their constitutional guarantee of Kashmiri semi-autonomy.

While we saw no demonstrations or anything frightening, most shops the Kashmiris deemed "non-essential" were closed, except for two hours in the early morning. Most restaurants were closed and no local transportation was running—no buses, no trains, not even any tuk-tuks (motorized rickshaws). Nothing. We were lucky that we'd booked a car and driver ahead of time.

Since it was Friday, the holiest day of the week for Muslims, when demonstrations might break out following afternoon prayers at the mosques downtown, ten miles away in the "old city," we postponed our included mosque visit there on our guide's advice. As any demonstrations would take place far from the lake itself though, we drove to see other sites near the lake instead.

As I was now ready to shop for some locally made handicrafts and clothes, our guide arranged for a large shop to quietly open just for us. On display were large selections of crewel embroidered men's and women's clothing, colorful handwoven carpets, and near weightless Pashmina shawls, which are made from the fine cashmere goat fur. (The word "cashmere" is an Anglicization of the original "Kashmir.") There were also bedspreads and intricately painted papier-mâché trays, coasters, small animals and boxes. (Papier-mâché, a Kashmiri specialty dating back more than 1,000 years, is made by soaking paper, drying it in a mold, painting it with intricate patterns, then lacquering it.)

I picked out six three-inch high adorable smiley-faced papier-mâché cats to give as gifts. They were something unique and were very well crafted, but the prices seemed astronomical compared to Kashmiri goods I'd seen before. Even with the small discount offered, the prices were too high. As the shopkeepers didn't seem amenable to any serious bargaining, we sadly left empty handed. We'd just arrived and were confident that we'd be able to find other desirable hand-made products later in our trip.

We then drove to nearby Shankaracharya Mandir, a prominent Hindu Shiva temple and the Kashmir Valley's oldest shrine, said to be built over the ruins of a second century BC temple. It was perched 1000 feet above the city. At the base of the 3½ mile uphill access road there was an army checkpoint, where we were asked to show our passports. No problem. We would have liked to have continued up the hill on foot, but we were warned against walking this stretch because of bears which lived nearby in the thick forests.

At the top of the road we stopped at a second army checkpoint, where we were asked politely to get out of the car, and were told to leave our camera and cell phones in the car with our driver. This was because this temple was deemed to be especially sacred, and, as such, total quiet must be maintained. The temple was readily accessed by a wide gray stone block 263 step stairway, and it only took ten minutes for me to climb to the top. My husband, who's always averse to any serious climbing, stayed behind. After seeing a large lingum at the entrance, a Shiva symbol of vitality, I was invited by a Hindu priest sitting inside to come inside the small revered temple. It smelled of incense, and he offered a prayer. It was a very peaceful moment.

After getting our camera and phones back at the top checkpoint, we saw a break in the trees, where there was a commanding view of 500 or more houseboats bunched together on Dal Lake. We also saw many tin-roofed buildings on land, including some that looked like alpine chalets. Quite a few sported satellite dishes. Although it was hazy, we took lots of photos, and saw more houseboats with funky names like Sans Souci (no worries), New Sans Souci (new no worries), Australia, New Sydney, New Melbourne, Malaya, and Rolex. It was fun just seeing how creative some of the names were.

Houseboats moored on Dal Lake

The houseboats have interesting names

The interior of Shalimar Bagh's pavilion

Mystique dahlias in Shalimar Bagh

Amazing Mughal architecture

Next we explored two famous Mughal gardens lying along Dal Lake's eastern shore. Both Shalimar Bagh and Nishat Bagh, (Bagh meaning enclosed garden), had similar features–huge leafy stately plane trees with brilliant fall colors, flower beds of vibrant red and yellow mystique dalhias and pink king's crown, arched pavilions, waterfalls and watercourses, terraced lawns, walkways, and sculpted arched walls.

Shalimar Bagh's pavilion

Shalimar Bagh, meaning "abode of love," was built in 1619 by Emperor Jahangir for his wife Noor Jahan as a pleasure garden. It's pavilion had stunning black marble pillars and black and gold painted floral arches.

View of the gardens from Shalimar Bagh's pavilion

Nishat Bagh, "Gardens of Gladness," three miles away, designed by Noor Jahan's brother in 1633, was larger than Shalimar Bagh and had steeper and more dramatic terraces and waterfalls. Even though the fountains weren't working, we loved the flowing waterfalls, the lakeside setting, and the Mughal architecture, which had first come to India from Eastern Turkey, Persia and Central Asia in the early 1500s. The steep terraces and a central water channel were sandwiched between the lake and the hills.

Nishat Bagh

We also appreciated seeing that the entrance fees to the gardens were so low, the equivalent of 28 cents for adults, that local people could afford to come enjoy them. Also the charge for foreigners here was the same as it was for Indian nationals, which was refreshing, as so many sites visited in

India charge foreigners much more than they charge Indians. We had seen so many remarkable things already today, and the morning wasn't even over yet.

We drove around for quite a while looking for an open lunch restaurant in order to enjoy a late lunch, but to no avail. Every restaurant we tried was closed, due to the protest strike. Thankfully we'd always brought snacks with us in the car, which tided us over.

Then we finally found an open restaurant, Lhasa, whose hidden back door was opened for us, but their front door was closed, in order to appear to be completely adhering to the strike. We, and a handful of other foreigners, sat in a pretty garden with blooming rose bushes. (Aside from the other foreigners we saw here, we saw no others, albeit there were quite a few non-Kashmiri Indians, including some that seemed to be on their honeymoons.)

There were no Kashmiri customers here, as they were honoring the protest. Lhasa Restaurant is "multi-cuisine," offering vegetarian and non-vegetarian Kashmiri, Indian, Tibetan and Chinese food. We ordered Tibetan vegetable momos (steamed dumplings), and a tasty Kashmiri chicken dish, and paid the equivalent of US $8. We'd brought our own bottled water in from the car, which our guide Majid said was OK to do in restaurants. That way we knew it would be safe to drink. The only drawback to Lhasa was the squat toilet, which consisted of a small hole in the ground with foot pads on either side. It was cleaner than most Western-style toilets in India, but it was still a challenge. (Hint: Practice your squatting exercises before leaving home.)

Lhasa Restaurant in Srinagar

Then it was time to head back to our houseboat to relax on the verandah. We'd enjoyed our day out sightseeing, especially the many encounters we had with local Kashmiris. So many spoke good English and wanted to talk to us, and they often even asked if they could have their photos taken with us. At times it felt like we were the tourist attraction! The local Kashmiris weren't reticent about discussing the current political impasse, but we didn't sense that anyone felt hopeful that their situation would change for the better any time soon. We had many conversations with them about the self-imposed boycott, which they'd instituted because it seemed that they felt powerless to do much else. The biggest concern they expressed was that the dissolution of their special status would now allow non-Kashmiris to buy land and push forward with development in Kashmir. This hadn't been allowed before. Peoples' greatest fear seemed to be the potential loss of their cherished traditional culture.

When we traveled we were often asked the usual question, "Where are you from?" "California," we answered. We'd hoped to avoid conversations about American politics, and saying California rather than the United States somehow seemed to work. But, even more frequently, we were now asked how old we were. Really? Yikes! That now seemed to often be the first question. People seemed amazed that any older people were there, traveling freely and happily on their own.

Relaxing on Mahjong's verandah

A day trip to Pahalgam

It was time, on our third day, to head to the countryside for the day. We drove southeast on a 56 mile stretch of good paved, double-lane, almost traffic-free roads through the fertile Kashmir Valley toward Pahalgam.

We saw village after village where life seemed to be going on as usual. People walked to market or rode horses with colorful cloth saddles, shepherds tended their sheep, and groups of women washed clothes in a communal stream.

Even though it was fairly warm out, they dressed conservatively, but no women had covered faces or *burqas*. Many wore scarves over their heads. (The Kashmiri population is 97% Muslim, and most follow a mystical non-fundamentalist type of Islam, one which originated in ancient Persia.)

Half an hour after leaving Srinagar we happened upon large fields of purple saffron crocus flowers. We'd arrived in Pampore, the center of Kashmir's renowned saffron industry, where saffron has been cultivated since the 10th century.

We stopped, got out of the car, and walked through a field. There we saw a Kashmiri man picking the purple saffron flowers and putting them in a plastic basket. We approached him and he handed us a saffron flower. Each flower has three red anthers, the only parts used for the spice.

It takes more than forty-five hundred blooms to yield just one ounce of this most expensive spice in the world. He had a great smile and was happy to have his photo taken. We felt lucky to have had such good timing, as the saffron flower only blooms in late autumn.

A saffron flower harvest in Pampore

Crocus blossom

Then we drove to Anantnag. Throughout the valley we frequently saw military checkpoints and bunkers. The Indian army soldiers, many of whom were said to have been recruited from the poorest villages in India, appeared bored and non-threatening. Apparently many had joined the army so they'd be guaranteed enough food and housing.

We visited the Anantnag Sulphur Spring, a large natural hot spring pool with unpolluted clear water. The pool and the thousands of fish teeming in it are all sacred to the small surrounding Hindu communities. A priest from the adjoining Hindu temple, Mattan Temple, greeted us and answered our many questions. There was also a Sikh temple (gurdwara) adjoining the Hindu temple. A sign at the entrance to the complex, written in four languages, said, "VISITORS HAVING DONE NON-VEGETERIAN BREAKFAST/LUNCH SHOULD NOT ENTER THE TEMPEL & HOLY SPRINGS." Luckily we'd had a vegetarian breakfast.

Anantnag sulphur spring

A sign at the entrance to the sulphur spring

Women washing clothes at the spring

We continued to Pahalgam, a name meaning village of shepherds. It is a resort town and popular mountain retreat an hour further down the road at 7000 feet elevation, on the slopes of the Himalayas. It is crisscrossed by two rivers, has snow-capped mountains, sleepy valleys and dense forests of giant conifers and pines. Many Indian films are made here. We saw dozens of inviting attractive summer vacation cottages lining the Lidder River, and signs advertising white water rafting. We then enjoyed a long walk in the fresh mountain air. As we saw no one around, it felt like we could enjoy the scenery quietly by ourselves. But I put white water rafting and coming back in the summer on my "to do" list for next time.

On the way home we stopped again in Anantnag at a small bakery and ordered hot baked chicken pot pies and a box of homemade candy to eat for a late lunch on our houseboat, and to share with our houseboat man. The pies were delicious, but the candy was inedible. We have no idea what it was. Mystery food!

We also stopped at the Avantipur ruins to see vestiges of the region's pre-Islamic past. Little however remained of the dual Hindu temples, which dated from the 9th century. Some small stones had sculptures on them, but unfortunately there was little still intact to see or appreciate.

Local Kashmiris en route to Pahalgam

A journey to Sonamarg

On our fourth day we started out early for a full day trip to see Sonamarg, "meadows of gold," a mountain village and alpine resort of only 1,000 inhabitants, 49 miles northeast of Srinagar.

Sonamarg is Kashmir's last town before reaching the treacherous, narrow, winding but exhilarating Zoji La pass leading to Ladakh.

Sitting at 9,000 feet elevation, Sonamarg is occupied mostly in the summer, but it is also a ski resort in the winter. Due to the 3,800 foot climb up from Srinagar, on roads snaking through massive mountains, the drive took two hours.

On arrival we saw that we were in a valley immediately surrounded by tall mountain peaks and forests of fir and pine trees. We were more than happy to find clean Western-style restrooms at a small hotel where we'd parked.

Our guide Majid asked if we wanted to ride horses up to the nearby Thajiwas glacier. I was more than up for it, but my husband was not. I paid about $12 for the two-hour trip and was accompanied by a young teenage horseman who walked with me while I rode the well-cared-for gentle animal that he'd chosen for me.

The climb started on a wide walking trail, where a number of hikers were trekking uphill as I rode. Then the trail flattened out to a long narrow valley, followed by a steeper incline. My horse crossed creeks and stepped sure-footedly on one large stone after the other on the climb up. Soon there was no longer a discernible path, and after a while the number of hikers I saw had dwindled to just a few.

Trekkers on the trail to the Thajiwas glacier

Suzanne's horse on the way up to Thajiwas glacier

Suzanne on horseback close to the Thajiwas glacier

We stopped from time to time so, at the suggestion of my horse guide, I could take photos of the majestic mountains and pine trees that surrounded me and of the glacier in the distance. He often told me, in good English, what we were seeing.

He was very patient and kind. Since it had been quite a while since I'd ridden a horse, I was grateful that he'd accompanied me as we climbed steep often uneven very rocky terrain, descended some, and then climbed again. Often there were no clear paths.

Soon even the sounds of the village of Sonamarg below us vanished and there was complete stillness, complete quiet, all something so rare to feel in India. After riding for about another hour more we reached a very flat expansive green pasture. There I saw dozens of well tended beautiful for-hire horses, a few horsemen, and the glacier right in front of me.

The fresh air smelled delightfully of pine. I dismounted, grabbed a snack from my daypack, and walked alone toward the glacier. Magnificent!

Thajiwas glacier

On the walk back to the horse camp I found my horse guide in a tent, where a number of other local horse guides were eating lunch. One was intently smoking a hookah, a tobacco water pipe. I didn't try to join them, as they were all local men who were enjoying eating and talking together.

More riders started to show up, and by the

Horse guides

time we headed back down the hill there were dozens of gleeful, talkative, often loud, Indian tourists on horseback who broke the silence. I was happy that we'd started out early.

Horse camp near the glacier

After we got back to the small hotel at the bottom of the hill, my horse guide very politely asked for his tip: "Have I shown you a nice experience?" Indeed he had. I gave him the equivalent of $3.00, which was more than the recommended amount, and he seemed really happy with that.

Clearly small amounts of money, which make little or no difference to many of us in our lives, make a big difference to people in this part of the world. I only hoped that I wasn't his only customer that day.

My husband and I were the only diners for lunch in the small hotel's restaurant. We looked forward to ordering trout, a local specialty, as the rivers here were reported to be teeming with them. But the waiter told us "Sorry, no trout." We poured over the copious menu and ordered other dishes. "Sorry, don't have."

Then we learned, because we were at the very end of the summer tourist season, and because most tourism had been cut off by the Indian government, that they only had two items available from their menu. Fortunately we'd learned to love dal, a dish of lentils or split peas to which spices and water are added, and then the ingredients are simmered to make a thick soup.

Due to time constraints we didn't explore any of the many opportunities for nature walks or longer treks. These might best be done in late spring and early summer, because then the whole Kashmir valley is covered in flowers.

On the road back to Srinagar we stopped at Kashmir Art Mahal, a large emporium packed wall-to-wall with colorful Kashmiri handicrafts. A friendly, helpful, and thankfully not pushy proprietor showed us, among countless other things, a good selection of reasonably priced good quality small papier-mâché cats, and we bought four at about $4 each, as well as an embroidered dress for $9.

Papier-mâché cats

Suzanne's embroidered Kashmiri dress

I was amazed at how much craftsmanship went into each item and hoped, given the low prices, that the makers were still able to earn at least a sustainable living. As I didn't know how to tell the difference between the higher quality of items like the locally made carpets and Pashmina shawls and the lesser quality ones made outside Kashmir and passed off as Kashmiri, I didn't buy anything else. But the tour of the showroom was a visual feast. There seemed to be thousands of beautiful items.

Once back in Srinagar we visited the stunning Saracenic style white marble Hazratbal mosque in the old town. It has a dome and just one minaret, and it is said to house a hair from prophet Mohammed's beard, a sacred relic. About a dozen women were praying outside on an expansive lawn. They stood in a row, facing the mosque. The women had a separate entrance to the mosque behind a curtain, as Muslim men and women always pray separately. As non-Muslims we weren't permitted entry, but we appreciated seeing the stunning exterior.

Hazratbal mosque in Srinagar's old town

This day had been the best so far. Back on our houseboat we checked up on international news on TV, bought two very small containers of the highly prized Pampore saffron from our houseboat man Ahmad for $5 each, and had more in-depth conversations with him.

He told us that the boat had no bookings after ours, and that it had had none long before ours. He said that after we left he'd hoped to be able to go see his wife and children, who lived far out of town. But as no local transportation was running, he feared that he couldn't go. At least he had somewhere to live and we got the impression that the tour company that employed him would help take care of him. We certainly hoped so.

Our final day: still more to see

After another delicious breakfast we sadly said goodbye to our houseboat man Ahmad, our shikara man Gulhar, and our cook. We asked Ahmad for his cell phone number in the hope of being able to contact him once phone calls were allowed again by the Indian government.

We took a quick photo of Ahmad and Gulhar, a prized picture, and handed each of them their tips for our stay. We put the Indian rupees for each in separate envelopes along with thank you notes which we wrote on postcards we'd brought from home that had photos of our hometown of Palm Springs, California. Although the tips suggested by the tour company were about $14 each for Ahmad and Gulhar and $12 for our cook, we gave Ahmad and Gulhar considerably more—$57 for Ahmad, $21 for Gulhar and $14 for our cook.

There was never even a hint from any of them that they should even be tipped. Even with that, we couldn't imagine how much they must struggle to earn a living. We just hoped we could make a difference, however small.

Then, sadly, we set off on our last shikara ride through the narrow canals to the jetty. Our car and driver were waiting. We handed them their tip envelopes. As we hadn't been thrilled with them, we tipped them just the suggested amount, $50 for our guide Majid and $40 for our driver Mehraj.

While Majid had been good on most of the logistics, he'd told us next to nothing about what we were seeing, and he often didn't come with us into the sites or shops we visited. While in the car they talked frequently to each other, but they rarely talked to us.

Gulhar (left) and Ahmad (right) in front of our houseboat

We'd striven to learn all we could about Kashmir and had learned a lot, but in large part what we learned hadn't been from them.

Before heading to the airport for a mid-afternoon flight back to New Delhi, we had time for one last treat, a visit to Srinagar's old town and the historic fourteenth century Khanqah Shah-i-Hamadan wooden mosque.

The old town, which emanates from the mosque, and which hugs the Jhelum River, is primarily comprised of eighteenth and nineteenth century wooden buildings. But since political strife and the resulting economic damage has marred the area for so long, many buildings were in various states of decrepitude. Many looked like they'd been fine houses or shops at one time, but now many even seemed deserted.

Srinagar's old town

Nothing gave us the impression that we lived in a modern age except for some parked cars and the usual massive tangle of overhead electrical wires marring the landscape.

The scene was more reminiscent of a town in Central Asia than one in more "modern" India. Very little looked open except for some cell phone stores, a mobile phone repair shop, a travel agency, pharmacies, and doctors offices, including "Dr. Singh, Super Specialist."

In order to visit the mosque I'd worn long pants, as shorts are not acceptable for women in Muslim Kashmir. I donned a large head scarf in order to respectfully visit the mosque, even though, as a non-Muslim, I would only be allowed to enter the courtyard to see the exterior. We'd put off the visit until today in order to avoid being there on a Friday, the Muslim's holiest day of prayer, which was the original day that had been planned for our visit.

The mosque, built to honor the Persian sufi who'd peacefully converted the region to Islamic mysticism in the

The Khanqah Shah-i-Hamadan mosque entrance in old town Srinagar

fourteenth century, served as both a prayer hall and a meeting hall. Originally constructed in 1395 but destroyed by fire, it was rebuilt in the 1730s, all without using any nails.

Although we knew that non-Muslims couldn't enter, we were happy to be invited to look through the open doorway and to peer through two very large front windows. The man sitting at the "construction fund" donation box at the entrance smiled at us and seemed welcoming, and he didn't ask us for any donations. When we respectfully left our shoes at the bottom of the steps leading up to the entrance no one asked for money to "guard our shoes" either. Refreshing! The entryway had ornate tile work, and painted papier-mâché covered much of the exterior as well.

The Khanqah Shah-i-Hamadan mosque exterior

The papier-mâché entrance walls

The Khanqah Shah-i-Hamadan mosque interior

As I peered through one of the large windows I asked if I could take photos. It was allowed and I could see and photograph the mosque's sparkling interior, which was replete with dazzling European chandeliers, stained glass windows, colorful lacquered papier-mâché covered columns and painted walls. What a sight to behold!

As it was a Monday, there were few worshipers. As we walked behind the mosque we noticed a woman clad in a black *burqa*, the only one we'd seen anywhere in Kashmir. The setting was quiet and peaceful, there was no sign of any imminent insurgency, and we saw no soldiers here.

Due to time constraints we skipped lunch and headed the 10 miles to Srinagar's airport, which had been expanded and modernized in 2009. As we didn't know exactly what to expect, we wanted to be there three hours before our flight back to New Delhi. We were glad we did, because this time security had been beefed up.

The airport lay three quarters of a mile behind a security checkpoint, where our car was checked—the inside, trunk and underneath. We were then asked politely to get out of the car, show our passports and e-tickets, and have our bodies and baggage carefully screened. Although there were long lines, the process only took about 20 minutes. The screeners were friendly, non-threatening, and efficient.

When our car reached the terminal building we said goodbye to our guide Majid and our driver Mehraj, and then showed our passports and e-tickets again in order to enter the building. There our bodies and bags were screened again. (As in most Indian airports, bags are first screened as soon as you enter.) Fine with us. We'd arrived in plenty of time.

The flight on IndiGo airlines on a modern plane was well organized, and quiet. Yet when I peered out my window for a last look, I experienced only an intense sadness. Would the Kashmiri people be OK? Would the beauty of this place remain the same? Would I ever return?

An hour and forty minutes later we landed in New Delhi and were back in "modern" India. A trip of a lifetime? Absolutely.

Final thoughts

We were often told to come back in the summer, "tourist season," when things promised to be more lively. We'd missed seeing Jama Masjid, Srinagar's largest mosque, with a capacity of 33,333 worshipers, which was closed. We didn't get to enjoy a sunset view over Srinagar from the Hari Parbat fort because the road to it was closed. We didn't get to experience walking through the old bazaar or get to visit the early morning floating vegetable market. And we couldn't arrange a Wazwan, the traditional 36 course banquet.

We didn't see the ski resort of Gulmarg or take the gondola cable car up the mountain there, as it's best visited in winter. Nor did we visit the Sri Amarnath Cave Temple near Pahalgam, a natural occurrence and one of Hinduism's holiest pilgrimage sites, as the pilgrimages occur only in July and August and we were non-Hindu.

So there was always the possibility of a hoped-for return if things remained safe and more things opened up. There were still so many wonderful things to see and do.

Yet, despite these disappointments, I was happy that the original planned September tour to Kashmir hadn't come to fruition. That itinerary hadn't included Sonamarg, a trip highlight, and as it was a less desirable, shorter, and faster-paced itinerary as well, I would have missed so many things. And since my husband hadn't signed up for the original tour he wouldn't have come to know and enjoy Kashmir at all. The blissful days we spent together in Kashmir ended up costing us only $1254 for everything. Had we stayed home we might have spent even more. So, in an odd way, coming to Kashmir might have even saved us money!

Kashmir turned out to be more special than I'd even imagined, and my expectations at the outset had been especially high. Kashmir turned out to be a peaceful serene respite from the often deafening sounds of "modern" India, its crowds, its trash, its beggars, and its seeming chaos. Even though I loved all of India passionately, it was at times taxing. Furthermore, in Kashmir, as a foreign visitor and not a Kashmiri, the military presence felt surprisingly reassuring and never oppressive. I never felt unsafe, not even for a moment. (Clearly the experience of a local Kashmiri might feel very different.)

Kashmir was and remains surely one of earth's most beautiful, most romantic and most serene places. An inscription on a wall of the Shalimar gardens pavilion, attributed to its founder Emperor Jahangir, says, "If there is a paradise on the earth, it is here; it is here; it is here."

I learned so much about Kashmiri culture from what I saw and from the many conversations I had with local people. I gained an even greater appreciation of Muslim craftsmanship, architecture, and traditions than I'd had before coming.

Most importantly, I'd added to my life's lessons, those of a never-ending search for beauty, for peace, and for understanding. Kashmir! Yes, I'd fallen in love.

Afterword

While Kashmir has the largest Muslim population in the world without its own country, Indian Prime Minister Modi's expressed justification for stripping Kashmir's special status was his government's desire to bring development to an area with huge unemployment. (In India Muslims on average are poorer than Hindus, and are less well educated.) Yet many Kashmiris believe that Modi's real intent is to reverse the area's Muslim majority by now allowing non-Muslims to permanently reside in the area. They fear that India's actions will turn them into a minority in their own land.

Article 35A of the Indian constitution, now also repealed, had given only Kashmiris the right to government jobs, scholarships and land ownership in Kashmir. Outsiders weren't allowed to settle there permanently.

The scrapping of this article engendered a new Indian central government issued domicile law. This law states that anyone who's lived in Kashmir for at least 15 years and who has the required level of high school education can apply for a domicile certificate. The certificate would grant them permanent residency and entitle them to government jobs in the region. Children of Indian government employees who'd worked in Kashmir for at least 10 years could also now claim these rights.

Since May 18, 2020, domicile certificates were granted to up to 25,000 people, with more to come. Many of the new "permanent residents" were Hindu refugees who'd come to live in Kashmir when the Indian subcontinent was partitioned in 1947. The whole situation remains extremely complicated.

On orders from the Indian central government the local government in Kashmir was forced to issue large numbers of domicile certificates quickly. But as there wasn't enough time to verify applicants' claims, the whole process raised suspicion.

The certificates were issued in spite of statements from important foreign leaders such as President Joe Biden, who insists that India restore the rights of the Kashmiri people. Most Kashmiris themselves realize that little can now be done. Even the Kashmiri-instituted "strike," which further damaged commerce, seems to have been unable to effect any critical rollback.

Most ethnic Kashmiris feel totally alienated from India's central government, and many, if not most, don't feel that they're Indian at all. Some want Kashmir to join Muslim Pakistan, while others want to have their own country, with complete independence.

Rebel groups, some of which are supported by the Pakistani government, enjoy broad-based popularity throughout the Kashmir Valley. There has long been an armed movement, although the vast majority of Kashmiris aren't part of it, and it hasn't succeeded. We saw no signs of any imminent insurgency, or even any demonstrations, although nothing was hidden from us. While the political situation remains unsettled, as it has been for the last 73 years, a solution seems to be only a distant prospect.

The most dramatic changes likely to occur now are perhaps those related to economic development. Will high-rise luxury hotels and more modern housing now be built? Will the non-Muslim population increase dramatically? Will looming increased regional economic prosperity, better employment and a rise in the standard of living significantly benefit the Kashmiri people? Or will new building just mar the pristine landscape? Will the influx of more non-Muslims create more conflict or lead perhaps to more harmony and understanding?

Will Kashmiris have more choices and more amenities? And, if so, will these changes make them happier? Or will development threaten the centuries old traditions that have made Kashmir such a unique and special place?

As I don't know what change will bring, I was glad I went now. If I go back, it will be as soon as possible, if the security situation remains stable. If it does, don't even hesitate to go. You too are likely to fall in love with Kashmir!

Essential travel information

A note about Covid-19

I was lucky to have left before the Covid-19 pandemic ravaged India, as clearly it isn't safe or even permitted to go there now. Yet now's the perfect time to start planning your trip, so that as soon as it's advisable to go, you'll be ready. Do your "homework" now. Read all you can from the resources I've provided and others. Make a budget, and decide what season you'd prefer to go in. Check out possible tour companies. See who might want to travel with you, and which airlines you might take. Decide what handicrafts you might want to buy in Kashmir and learn more about them. Will you want to visit other parts of India as well? How much time will you have for your trip? What type of visa would work best for you? Buy a money belt, daypack and a reliable suitcase if you don't already have them. If you're now self-quarantining at home, this "project" will be a fun one, and you'll quickly find joy in something exciting to look forward to. When times are right again, you'll be ready to go.

Resources

Tour operator

The tour company and agent I used, Rajinder, of The Travel Circuit located in New Delhi, can be reached by e-mail **Rajinder@travelcircuit.in**. The company's phone is (91) 11.41649917. Rajinder's cell phone is (91) 9810491010. The Travel Circuit is a large company and the contacts I had with their other agents were also exemplary. They accept payment by bank transfer or credit card. RSV TravelCircuit Pvt. Ltd. #207 Allied House #1, L.S.C. Pushp Vihar, New Delhi 110062 India. Their website is **www.thetravelcircuit.com**.

Travel insurance

The travel insurance company I've used happily for many years is Travel Insurance Center, (866) 979-6753. 8420 W. Dodge Rd., Suite 510, Omaha, NE 68114. Contact: Dan Drennan. **Dan@travelinsurancecenter.com**. The other agents there also do an excellent job. They offer honest advice and fair prices.

Books and magazines

International Travel News is a monthly magazine written by subscribers and editors who provide detailed information on foreign destinations in an up-close-and-personal format without hype or glitz. They offer potential subscribers a free sample copy. (800) 486-4968, **www.intltravelnews.com**, **info@intltravelnews.com**, 8300 Fair Oaks Blvd., Ste. 405, Carmichael, CA 95608. My top pick!

Culture Smart! India: the essential guide to customs and culture is an excellent book which provides insights and advice.

DK Eyewitness India © 2019 has only a few pages about Kashmir specifically, but it has beautiful well-formatted photographs and illustrations on all of India and some excellent advice, much of which is relevant to travel in Kashmir.

If you can read in a foreign language, often guidebooks written in these languages provide resources and insights not seen in many American guidebooks. If you speak French, for example, the Routard Guides, available at **Amazon.com**, give down-to-earth practical advice for budget and mid-range travelers.

If you'll be in New Delhi stop by Amrit Book Company, N21 Connaught Circus Rd, Block N, Connaught Place. They offer a huge selection—a feast for book lovers.

Newspapers printed in English
Times of India (in print and **www.indiatimes.com**)

Hindustan Times (in print and **www.hindustantimes.com**)

Kashmir Times (in print and **www.kashmirtimes.com**)

Online Resources
Aljazeera.com, also available as a television channel in India, can be relied upon for up-to-date unbiased information. You can also put their app on your phone. Go to Google's Play Store or Apple's App Store and search for Al Jazeera.

JKTourism.jk.gov.in, the official website of the Jammu and Kashmir Department of Tourism, is rich in resources and suggestions.

Greaterkashmir.com also offers valuable information.

IndiaMike.com has a travel forum.

LonelyPlanet.com also has a travel forum, which you can access at **www.lonelyplanet.com/thorntree/welcome**, then click on "Select country," scroll down and select India, then search the forum for any recent comments on Kashmir.

Government advisories
Both the U.S. State Department and governments of other English speaking countries have websites to check for safety and security advice and for any warnings before committing to any foreign trip. I don't rely on the U.S. State Department's information alone, but rather, I view advice from several governments in combination before making any international travel decisions.

For the U.S. State Department, go to **travel.state.gov**, click on "International Travel", type the country's name in the search bar on the left side of the page, then click on "India Travel Advisory" on the page that comes up. There are now four levels that can be assigned to a country:

Level	Advisory
1	Take normal precautions
2	Take increased precautions
3	Reconsider travel to that country
4	Do not travel to that country

For Canadian government assessments go to **travel.gc.ca/travelling/advisories**. For the United Kingdom go to gov.uk/foreign-travel-advice. For Australia view **smartraveller.gov.au**.

The free U.S. government's STEP, Smart Traveler Enrollment Program, is offered to U.S. citizens traveling abroad. It lets you enter information about your trips abroad so that the U.S. Department of State, via its embassies and consulates, can better assist you if there's an emergency at your destination. Sign up at **travel.state.gov**.

Safety and security

While it's always necessary to be vigilant, and there's never a guarantee that any trip can be taken with no risk whatsoever, there are a few important things to keep in mind when visiting Indian-administered Kashmir.

While the vast majority of Kashmiris are peaceful, there exists a small minority of extremist separatist groups, which are often encouraged by the Pakistani government. These separatists, many of whom want Kashmir to join Muslim Pakistan, killed several Hindu truck drivers who had arrived in October 2019 from outside Kashmir to deliver goods in the Anantnag district. These were isolated incidents which took place far from tourist areas and tourists have never been targeted.

The heavy visible military presence ordered by the Indian government, which includes stationing soldiers at almost every major intersection, made me feel safer, not less safe. No soldiers ever looked or acted aggressively and most looked more bored than anything else.

Use a reliable tour operator, who, through sub-contractors, will hire local guides and drivers, and who are best aware of up-to-date conditions. Conditions can change quickly day-to-day or, at times, hourly. Check local newspapers or newspaper websites, often available in English, for any security related headlines. And make sure the tour company you use tells you how to contact them, preferably 24/7. Get their local address in case the phones and internet are shut down or just aren't working.

Your tour company should tell you if there are any "hot spots," and they will avoid taking you to those areas. Some areas, like Srinagar's old town with its beautiful wooden mosques, are best avoided on Fridays for example, as Friday is the holiest day for Muslims. While any uprisings are rare in Kashmir, if they do happen, they are most likely to occur on Fridays. The crime rate for non-separatist related crimes is very low.

The Dal and Nagin Lake areas in Srinagar are far, about 10 miles, from the old town and are rarely affected by any security problems. Much of what there is to see and do in Srinagar is on or near these lakes.

As I've traveled alone for most of my life, I've learned how to look confident when walking in a public place. I keep a steady determined pace, as if I know exactly where I'm headed, even in cases where, in reality, I'm totally lost. If I need to look at a map or at my phone I go into a local business to do so, so I don't look vulnerable. If I need to find someone who speaks English to help me, I often head to the nearest pharmacy, as almost all pharmacists speak English.

Although violence against tourists in Kashmir is almost unheard of, petty theft occasionally occurs, even though I saw or heard of none while I was there. Wear a money belt hidden under your clothes which holds your passport, any tour vouchers, any large denominations of cash, your ATM card, credit card, important phone numbers and critical e-mail addresses. Keep duplicates of any important information in your locked suitcase. Before leaving home e-mail to yourself a copy of your passport's identity pages, visas, airline tickets and contact information.

Try to avoid accessing your money belt in public, especially if you're in a crowd. It's helpful to carry the equivalent of about $100, which you'll need in order to make small purchases and for emergencies. Keep it in a separate easier to access place, like a shirt or pants pocket, one which can be buttoned or zippered. This avoids you having to access your money belt when you just want to buy small things like fruit or coconut slices from street vendors. Also store your cell phone in a closeable secure pocket. If you're using a daypack in a public place always carry it in front of you rather than on your back.

Good quality comfortable money belts can be ordered online from **ricksteves.com**, **eaglecreek.com** and elsewhere. If you have lots of things to secure you may want to purchase travel shirts and pants from companies such as Clothing Arts **www.clothingarts.com**, which claims they are pickpocket proof.

If you can't book your Kashmir trip in its entirety before you arrive, a local travel agent in Srinagar can often make last-minute arrangements for you on the spot or you can contact any tour companies you've researched. Pay by credit card if at all possible, even if there is a small surcharge to do so. This gives you an added layer of protection if you don't receive what you've paid for. While I've never had this happen, it does give more peace of mind.

When to go

Most of Kashmir has a temperate climate in the Spring, Summer and Fall, but there's often heavy snowfall from December to February. Even India's summer monsoon, which produces heavy rainfall in much of the country, is moderate in Kashmir, with light to medium rainfall only, and usually only in July and August. Local travel agents advise coming between June and September. Because of the monsoon though the busiest months are May, June and October. Summer temperatures usually have highs in the mid 80s F, with an average of only six days of rain. We enjoyed traveling in

October, when temperatures were in the mid 70s and we had no rain.

Getting a visa

While, due to Covid-19, the Indian embassy and consulates in the U.S. aren't currently issuing tourist visas to most Americans and almost all travel to India is still banned, the following information may be useful in planning for a future trip when restrictions ease.

U.S. passport holders must always have an Indian visa before arriving in India. Your passport must be valid for a minimum of six months beyond the last day of your intended stay and it has to have at least two blank pages in it. You also must have an onward or return transportation ticket to a non-India destination.

Getting a visa may now be easier than ever, as more visa options are now available to apply for and receive online. While there are still regular standard paper visas available, e-visas are faster to obtain. When your application is accepted you'll receive an e-mail with the visa attached. Print it and show it when checking in for your flight to India. Then show it again upon arrival. When you arrive in India at a designated airport, seaport, or any permitted land entry point an immigration officer will put an e-visa stamp in your passport.

The most recently available e-visas are:
- 30 days, double entry, meaning once you arrive you can leave India and come back once, as long as your original entry and reentry stay combined don't exceed 30 days. This visa cannot be extended. The current cost is $26, as of March 2020, when they stopped issuing tourist visas.

- one year, multiple entry. The time period starts the date your visa is issued, not when you first arrive in India. The maximum stay during each visit is 180 days. The current cost is $41.

- five year, multiple entry. As with the one year visa, the time period starts the day your visa is issued, and the maximum stay during each visit is 180 days. The current cost is $82.

Kashmir's airport in Srinagar is currently a legal entry point to India in terms of passing through Indian immigration without stopping elsewhere in India first. As conditions could change at short notice however, always verify that this is still the case if this situation applies to you.

Visa information provided by the Indian government can be found at www.indianvisaonline.gov.in. There's a help desk at **indian-evisa@gov.in**. Phone: 1+(91) 11-24300666 direct to India.

Several commercial visa services also offer help if you apply for your visa through them, but additional fees apply.

When tourist visas are offered again, help can also often be obtained from the Indian Embassy in Washington, D.C. and from the various Indian Consulates located throughout the U.S.:

Indian Embassy in Washington, D.C.
   www.indianembassy.org (202) 939-7000

Consulates:
- San Francisco, CA **www.cgisf.org**   info@cgisf.org (415) 668-9764

- Chicago, IL www.indianconsulate.com
  hoc@indianconsulate.com (312) 595-0405

- New York, NY www.indiacgny.org cg@indiacgny.org
  (212) 774-0600

- Houston, TX www.cgihouston.org cgi-hou@swbell.net
  (713) 626-2148

- Atlanta, GA www.indianconsulateatlanta.org
  contact@indianconsulateatlanta.org (404) 963-5902

Kashmiri culture, beliefs, traditions, and practices

Predominantly Muslim Kashmir has a unique non-Arabic culture, which resulted from migrations of diverse peoples who came and settled over the past 1,000 years. Their monotheistic Islamic religion, which came in the 1400s, is predominantly of the Sufi tradition. This is a gentler, more humanist and more mystical faith than the more rigid one followed in countries such as Saudi Arabia. To Muslims their Islamic faith isn't just a religion, but it's an entire way of life, a code that clearly defines how to live and it is deeply ingrained. While Muslims are taught to pray five times a day, Friday is their holy day, when special prayers take place in mosques. Muslims do not eat pork or wear products that come from pigs, such as pigskin.

When you meet a Kashmiri (and many other North Indians as well) put the palms of your hands together and say, "Namaste," a form of hello which translates to "I bow to you." If you're encountering more than one person it's polite to greet the oldest appearing person first, as older people are highly respected here.

Older people are often called "uncle" and "auntie," a term of affection, even though they aren't usually the speaker's real uncles or aunts.

Another way to say, "Hello" is "As-Salaam-Alaikum," meaning "Peace be with you." Most local people are talkative and love to engage in conversations in English with foreigners. Kashmiris, and most Indians, are naturally curious, and they seek to start conversations with you. Some even want to practice their English. Don't be surprised if they ask you some very personal questions, questions not frequently asked in initial conversations in the West. Indians may do this in order to quickly ascertain your social status, which in turn tells them if and how to proceed. Frequent often intrusive questions might be about your profession, how much money you make, your marital status, your age, and about your family.

If you feel embarrassed just answer in vague terms or, if necessary, just make up something. And reciprocate by asking them about their family, which is always a welcome line of inquiry. You can even ask them to show you photos of their family members and you can show them yours, as well as photos of your home town, house or garden if they seem interested.

Most educated Indians like to debate and welcome hearing your opinions and ideas if they're well thought through.

Avoid discussing sex or anything else that can be embarrassing, such as poverty, the caste system or other Indian social problems. Saving face is very important, so never appear to be critical of India or bring up any potentially inflammatory political issue.

Although English is widely spoken in touristic areas, learning a few phrases in the local Kashmiri language, Koshur, will ingratiate you with locals. The ones I use the most are:

Hello	As-Salaam-Alaikum
Please	Meharbeunee
Thanks	Shukriya
Yes	Aa
No	Na
Where's the toilet/bathroom?	Taaylet kati ch'u

Kashmiris readily accept foreigners who are non-Muslims, and telling them you have a different religion is fine and can be talked about. Yet they are puzzled when someone tells them that they have no religion at all.

A life, even a simple life, filled with spirituality, social tolerance, harmony and good hospitality is seen as a successful one, rather than one just measured by monetary wealth. Indians have a strong belief in karma. Those with good karma, which is earned by doing good deeds, benefit from good consequences. Those with bad karma, which results from doing bad deeds, will suffer bad consequences.

Avoid speaking loudly or arguing. When I encounter a difficult situation which seems to be at an impasse, I just stand there silently, without moving, and just smile at them. For some reason this often results in a happy outcome.

Rather than make you unhappy though, they'll often tell you a "story," or even a lie. They rarely say, "No," but instead they'll say, "Maybe" or "I'll try." That usually means no. They'll rarely tell you that something you ask them for can't be done, as they consider that response to be rude. So they opt for non-committal, vague but friendly answers.

If someone offers you some food or a drink, it's polite to refuse at first, but then accept their second offer. Don't ever offer food from your plate or touch a communal dish with your left hand.

Shaking hands with someone of the opposite sex is viewed negatively, as is hugging, kissing or any other show of affection expressed by physical contact in public. The latter is sometimes even felt to be obscene. Men tend to keep a good distance away from women they aren't related to.

Don't be put off by Indians staring at you. At times I've felt like a zoo animal in India, subject to constant and unrelenting gazes and glares, but when I realized that this seemed to be almost a national pastime, it stopped bothering me. I experienced much less of this in Kashmir than in other parts of India however.

Many Indians find the practice of bathing in bathtubs disgusting, and opt for Western-style showers. Sometimes Indian showers are "bucket showers," where you fill a large plastic bucket they provide with water in a bathroom, pour it over your head, soap up, then rinse off with another filled bucket or two.

Likewise, many Indians find the use of toilet paper to be dirty, and they opt instead to clean with water, which they apply with a spray from a small "bidet" hose by the toilet. Then they use their left hand to dry themselves as best as possible. This is why only the right hand should be used when touching food, passing food or anything else to others or even touching anyone else with it. If you're a southpaw, this might be challenging.

Many toilets everywhere in India are "squat toilets" rather than Western-style sit down ones. Indians believe that their squat toilets are cleaner than Western ones. Before you use one remove everything from your pockets, as you risk losing it forever. Just place your feet on porcelain or dirt pads on either side of a hole in the ground and squat. A great sense of balance as well as some very strong thighs come in really handy here. Use the water from the spigot inside the stall to wash, then flush. If there's no flusher, there's usually a plastic pail in the stall to put water in, which you can then use to throw down the hole to flush.

While in Kashmir we had only Western-style showers and dealt with only one squat toilet, but amenities differ widely and depend on the type of accommodations you choose and the places you visit.

As feet are thought to be unclean, don't point them at anyone, and in places of worship, don't point them at any deity. Shoes should always be removed before entering a temple. If you're a Muslim and are therefore permitted to enter a Kashmiri mosque, shoes need to be removed here, just outside the entrance. Non-Muslims aren't allowed to go inside any mosque in Kashmir, and your shoes can be left on while walking around the exterior. If you're invited to someone's home, it's considered polite to ask your host whether or not to leave your shoes just outside the door. The same rule applies to your hotel room, guesthouse or houseboat during your stay in Kashmir. Sometimes socks are OK, such as inside mosques, so ask about those too.

At places of worship, and in most public places in Kashmir, women will be expected to have their shoulders, thighs, and legs covered, and at times even their heads. A long, wide scarf, called a *dupatta* in India, works well for women here, or you can bring your own scarf from home. A long ankle-length skirt, easily purchased or tailor-made in Kashmir or elsewhere in India, also works well here.

If you've been invited to a home or celebration outside the home and are bringing a gift, flowers are appreciated as long as they aren't white, as white flowers are used primarily at funerals. Sweets are always welcome as well. If the recipients are Muslim avoid giving anything containing alcohol or anything made from pigs.

Kashmiri food, food safety, and recipes

Kashmir has one of the most unique regional cuisines. As in many other Muslim regions, it is based on lamb. Muslims don't eat pork. The culinary tradition is heavily influenced by traders who came for centuries from Central Asia, China and Persia. Like much of North India, there is a preference for wheat-based foods such as breads, rather than rice-based ones. Aromatic whole spices are key ingredients in many of the most flavorful dishes. Most of the dishes we tasted everywhere in Kashmir were less firey and tongue-numbing than what we were served in most other places in India. There is a frequent use of yogurt (curd) and Kashmiri saffron.

Many restaurants offer both vegetarian (veg) and non-vegetarian (non-veg) options, while some are "pure veg" only. Vegetarian in India usually means no meat, no fish, and no eggs, yet there is no set definition.

Never drink tap water, and when showering, make sure not to let any get in your mouth. Use only bottled water, even for brushing your teeth, and before opening it, check that the seal is unbroken (not tampered with).

Avoid having ice in your drinks. But if you have to, try this trick: put the ice in a sandwich-sized plastic bag like a Ziploc, then set the bag in your drink. It works!

Make sure that hot dishes are served piping hot, and pass on eating salads, milk and un-peeled fruit. It's best to discretely wipe down cups, plates and utensils with 60 proof or higher alcohol before use.

While I had no "tummy problems" in Kashmir whatsoever, I've found over the years in traveling that the "culprit" can often be harmful bacteria on the banknotes we touch. So some pretty constant hand washing with soap and water or hand sanitizer really helps.

Recipes for the dishes we most enjoyed in Kashmir follow. They include Kashmiri tea (kahwa), Kashmiri lamb curry (rogan josh), chicken in yogurt sauce (chicken yakhni), and banana fritters. If you're unable to find some of the needed Indian spices locally, they can be ordered online from a choice of dozens of companies. Enjoy!

Kashmiri tea (Kahwa)
Ingredients
- 5 green tea leaves
- saffron (5 strands)
- 1 cinnamon stick
- 1 clove
- 1 cardamom
- ½ teaspoon dried rose petals
- dried fruits and nuts (almonds, apricots, raisins, dates, pineapple)

SUZANNE'S KASHMIR

Preparation
1. Heat 3 cups of water in a saucepan.
2. Add the cardamom, cinnamon stick, clove and the dried rose petals to the water.
3. Simmer for 5 minutes.
4. Add 5 saffron strands.
5. Remove the pan from the heat and add 5 green tea leaves.
6. Let it steep for 5 minutes, then strain.
7. Serve with the dried fruits and nuts.

Kasmiri lamb curry (Rogan Josh)
Ingredients
- 2¼ pounds of lamb (boneless or with bones in)
- fresh ginger
- 4 medium-sized shallots, thinly sliced
- 4 large garlic cloves
- cumin seeds
- black peppercorns
- black cardamom pods
- coriander seeds
- 1 clove
- 1 cinnamon stick
- turmeric
- fennel powder (saunf)
- red chili powder
- salt
- 16 oz. plain yogurt (not low-fat)
- vegetable or olive oil
- basmati rice

Preparation
1. Use a Dutch oven like Le Creuset or another heavy pan with high sides or a wok.

2. Roast 2 tsp. of cumin seeds, seeds from 9 cardamom pods, 2 tsp. coriander seeds, 3 black peppercorns, and the clove in a skillet without oil over low to medium heat until you smell the aroma. Be careful not to burn them.
3. Grind the roasted spices in a mortar and pestle.
4. Heat the Dutch oven, heavy pan or wok.
5. Add ¼ cup oil.
6. Add the 4 shallots.
7. Turn the flame to high and heat until the shallots are soft.
8. Cut the lamb into large bite-sized pieces and fry it over a medium flame until it's cooked through and browned throughout.
9. Add the roasted spices to the meat and shallots.
10. Heat for 5 minutes.
11. Grind a 1 inch piece of peeled and finely sliced ginger and 4 large garlic cloves in a mortar and pestle.
12. Add these to the pan and stir well, so that all the lamb is coated with these spices.
13. Add a cinnamon stick, 2 tsp. of turmeric, 2 tsp. of fennel powder and 1 tsp. red chili powder (or more, or less, to taste).
14. Stir and heat for another 3 minutes.
15. Stir the yogurt, then slowly add it, stirring it well into the other ingredients.
16. Add ¼ tsp. salt (or more, or less, to taste).
17. Heat on high for 2 minutes, then turn down the heat to simmer.
18. Cook for 60-90 minutes, stirring often, until the meat is tender.
19. Serve with basmati rice.

It makes about 4 servings.

Chicken Yakhni
Ingredients
- 2 pounds chicken thighs and legs
- 16 oz. plain yogurt (not low-fat)
- garlic paste
- ginger paste
- 3 green cardamoms
- 1 cinnamon stick
- salt
- black pepper
- mustard oil
- 1 small onion
- 4 garlic cloves
- fennel powder (saunf)
- ginger powder
- dried mint
- cumin
- vegetable oil

Preparation
1. Remove the skin from the chicken pieces.
2. Place the chicken in a sauté pan or other pan about 2" - 3" high.
3. Add 1 tsp. garlic paste, one tsp. ginger paste, and a pinch of salt to the chicken and stir.
4. Add 1 tsp. vegetable oil.
5. Cover and cook over a low (but not simmering) flame until completely cooked.
6. In a large saucepan blend 16 oz. of plain yogurt with 14 oz. of water.
7. Bring to a boil and stir.
8. Add 3 green cardamoms, the cinnamon stick, a small finely diced onion, 4 finely chopped garlic cloves, a pinch of salt and black pepper.

9. Turn down the flame to medium heat and reduce the volume by half, stirring often.
10. Add ¼ tsp. dried mint, ¼ tsp. ginger powder, ¼ tsp. black pepper, ½ tsp. fennel powder, and ¼ tsp. cumin.
11. Add the chicken to the pan with this sauce and stir.
12. Remove the pan from the flame.
13. Add more dried mint to taste.
14. Serve with basmati rice.

Banana fritters with raisins and powdered sugar
Ingredients
- 4 unripe bananas
- ¼ cup shredded unsweetened coconut
- ½ cup flour (all-purpose)
- ½ cup corn flour
- ¼ cup raisins
- 2 eggs
- powdered sugar
- vegetable oil
- ¼ tsp vanilla extract
- ¼ cup milk

Preparation
1. Make a batter by mixing the shredded coconut, milk, all-purpose flour, corn flour, eggs, vanilla, and raisins.
2. Slice each banana lengthwise into 3 horizontal strips.
3. Coat the strips with the batter.
4. Using a deep frying pan, deep fry the coated bananas in the vegetable oil until crispy and soft inside.
5. Remove the fritters from the pan and place on 3 layers of paper towels to absorb any excess oil.
6. Sprinkle with powdered sugar.
7. Serve with a side of mango, mint or tamarind chutney.

How to dress

If you want to try to fit in with the locals, do the best you can to dress like them.

As modest unrevealing dress is respectful of Muslim mores, avoid skimpy shorts on men and all shorts on women. Sleeveless tops, short skirts, anything tight-fitting or see-through should also be avoided when you're out in public. Jeans and T-shirts are sometimes considered unkempt in some public spaces, especially in the more conservative countryside. Men should wear shirts and pants, as these are culturally appropriate.

Most Indian-style garments are extremely comfortable. Even better is the fact that Indians love a lot of color, so cheery colorful clothes can be found almost anywhere. Also, wearing something where the colors seem to clash is never a problem, so there's no need for the things you choose to wear to all match.

Most Indian women, especially younger women, now wear *salwar kameez* rather than saris in their everyday lives. Saris are often kept for special celebrations and are sometimes considered odd if worn by foreigners. The *salwar kameez* outfit consists of a loose-fitting long and long-sleeved tunic called a *kurta* and baggy pants held up by a long drawstring. The *kurta*, sometimes also called a *dhoti*, can also be worn over Western-style pants or jeans. *Dupattas* are long scarves that come in beautiful colored patterns. They work well when draped over a T-shirt or blouse and can readily be used as a head or shoulder cover when visiting places of worship. Long skirts always work well, as they can be worn anywhere and are easier to deal with than pants when confronting a squat toilet.

What to bring—a packing list for Kashmir and all of India

At the left of each item I put a line (/) to first mark which items I want to take. Then, when I actually pack the item, I cross the / with a \ to make an X.

Luggage

_____   suitcase (I bring a 26" wheeled bag, which starts out half empty so I can fill it with colorful and fun purchases in India.)

_____   daypack

_____   3 TSA approved combination locks (1 for the suitcase, 1 for the daypack, and a spare)

_____   cable lock (to lock your daypack or suitcase to an overhead luggage rack when using long-distance buses or trains, or to something sturdy in a hotel room)

_____   a large, sturdy shopping bag

_____   3 luggage tags

_____   plastic bags (Ziploc or other brand; sandwich, quart and gallon sizes)

_____   hanging toiletries organizer (like the "wallaby" from Eagle Creek)

_____   small cloth organizers for toiletries, underwear, etc. (like the "Pack-It cubes" from Eagle Creek)

_____   small luggage scale (for flights within India, which have luggage weight limits, usually 33 pounds)

_____

_____

_____

Documents

Print copies of important documents rather than solely relying on those you've copied to your phone. (As my phone was stolen in India once, I learned this the hard way.)

_____ passport
_____ copies of your passport number, identity pages and Indian visa page
_____ passport photos
_____ airline tickets/e-tickets and copies
_____ printed itinerary and details
_____ contact information
_____ lodging reservations
_____ travel insurance company information
_____ destination information (what to see, do, etc.)
_____ maps
_____ credit cards and emergency phone numbers if your cards are lost or stolen
_____ debit (ATM) cards and emergency phone numbers if your cards are lost or stolen
_____ other important cards
_____ driver's license
_____ cash
_____
_____
_____

Electronics/electrical

_____ alarm clock, small (if not on your phone)
_____ camera, extra lenses, extra battery, battery charger, extra memory chips

_____ laptop computer or tablet (iPad or similar device), charger, SD card to USB adapter
_____ cell phone, charger
_____ flashlights
_____ electrical adapter plugs (to plug U.S. devices into Indian electrical sockets)
_____
_____
_____

Clothing

I try to bring garments that are 100% cotton, which are comfortable and work well when it's hot in India.

_____ 2 long sleeve shirts/blouses
_____ 2 short sleeve shirts/blouses
_____ turtleneck shirt
_____ jacket
_____ sweater
_____ ankle-length skirt
_____ 2 pair pants
_____ 1 pair jeans
_____ 1 pair warm-up pants and top (or pajamas)
_____ nightie
_____ bathrobe/beach cover-up
_____ bathing suit
_____ 7 pair undies
_____ 7 pair socks
_____ 2 handkerchiefs
_____ 2 bras (including 1 sports bra if you'll be on bumpy roads)
_____ belt

SUZANNE'S KASHMIR

_____ hat (like the Tilley hat)
_____ long scarf
_____ 1 pair long johns
_____
_____
_____

Security

_____ money belt
_____ fanny pack
_____

Shoes

_____ 1 pair walking shoes (e.g. from SAS) or sneakers
_____ 1 pair sandals (e.g. Teva or Ecco)
_____ 1 pair shower shoes
_____
_____

Laundry

_____ liquid detergent
_____ laundry bag
_____ small sewing kit
_____ universal sink stopper
_____ nylon clothes line
_____
_____

Eyeglasses

_____   1 pair you use every day
_____   1 back up pair
_____   1 pair sunglasses
_____   copy of your eyeglasses prescriptions
_____   eyeglasses cases
_____   eyeglasses cleaner cloth
_____
_____

Medicines/first aid

It's best to keep prescription medicines in their original bottles. Your pharmacist can help you split medicines which come in large bottles into smaller labeled ones. Photograph the prescription labels with your phone and print them out so you have copies. Always split your risk when you take critical medicines by putting some in your daypack, some in your suitcase, and a few in your money belt, along with a copy of the prescription.

Many commonly used non-prescription medicines like anti-diarrheals can be readily found at Indian pharmacies. Pharmacists often offer helpful advice as well.

_____   ace bandage
_____   anti-itch cream
_____   Band Aids (small and large)
_____   face masks
_____   feminine pads, tampons
_____   hand sanitizer
_____   Handi Wipes
_____   lozenges
_____   moleskin

_____ Neosporin
_____ prescription medicines
_____ vitamins
_____
_____
_____

Toiletries

Except in rural areas, many of these toiletries are readily available in India.

_____ bar of soap in a soap dish
_____ bobby pins
_____ Chapstick
_____ comb
_____ dental floss
_____ deodorant
_____ ear plugs
_____ eye shade
_____ Kleenex packets
_____ mosquito repellant with DEET (or buy Odomos brand in India)
_____ nail brush
_____ nail scissors
_____ Q-tips
_____ razors
_____ shampoo
_____ shower cap
_____ sunscreen (high strength)
_____ toilet paper (1 roll)

_____ toothbrush and holder
_____ toothpaste
_____ tweezers
_____
_____

Office supplies

I place these in gallon-sized ZipLoc bags.

_____ business cards
_____ #10 envelopes (for tips)
_____ 9" x 12" envelopes for receipts, destination information, etc.
_____ pads of writing paper (1 small, 1 large)
_____ paper clips (a few)
_____ pens
_____ photos of your family, home and pets
_____ post cards of your home town
_____ Post-It notes
_____ rubber bands (a few)
_____ sticky dots (to put on maps to plan itineraries)
_____ small pair of scissors
_____ trip journal, notebook, or steno pad
_____ yellow highlighter
_____
_____

Food

_____ almonds
_____ chicken pouches (that don't need refrigeration)
_____ dried fruit
_____ tea bags
_____ instant noodle soups

- _____ Kind bars
- _____ peanut butter cups (that don't need refrigeration)
- _____ Starbucks instant coffee packets
- _____ trail mix
- _____ vacuum-sealed tuna (that doesn't need refrigeration)
- _____
- _____

Food utensils

- _____ cloth napkin (thin)
- _____ plastic bowl/plate
- _____ plastic cup
- _____ plastic knife, forks, spoons
- _____ small bottle of alcohol (e.g. vodka, minimum 60 proof, for sterilizing eating utensils)
- _____ Swiss Army knife
- _____ water bottle (reusable)
- _____

Miscellaneous

- _____ books/printed games (e.g. Sudoku)
- _____ jewelry (non-valuable)
- _____ house keys
- _____ umbrella
- _____ watch
- _____ duct tape (a small amount wrapped around a small pencil, tongue depressor or dowel)
- _____ thin towel
- _____ pillowcase (to stuff your jacket in to use as a pillow where needed)

What to shop for and how to bargain

Kashmir offers many unique high quality traditional handicrafts made with expert craftsmanship. Many come from the Persian tradition, whose crafts and carpet making traditions date from the 15th century and were introduced to Kashmir when it was a key import and export center on a trans-Himalayan trade route.

If you're visiting New Delhi before heading to Kashmir, visit the Kashmir Government Arts Emporium. On display are hundreds of Kashmiri products, all with fixed prices. Most importantly, the sales people can tell you how each product is made, you can see what types of goods are on offer, and you can learn how to tell if something's well crafted. Also, knowing the prices the Emporium charges will give you an idea of pricing when you arrive in Kashmir. And you'll be more likely to know if what you're thinking about buying is of good quality. Emporium Building, A-7, Baba Kharak Singh Rd., opposite Hanuman Mandir, New Delhi, phone (91) 11.2336 4723.

Key buys in Kashmir

- Silky Pashmina shawls, which are woven from wool from nomadic cashmere goats and have intricate patterns. This skill is passed down from generation to generation. (Beware of cheaper imitations, which are made of cotton blends or silks.)

- Hand-knotted oriental rugs and carpets, which are made on traditional wooden looms, some of which take four years to finish, and are made of silk or wool, or a combination of both

- Felted crewel embroidered area rugs, which often have floral patterns

- Embroidered crewel cushions, bedspreads and curtains

- Handmade willow cricket bats

- Papier-mâché boxes, coasters, small animal figures, and other decorative items

- Dried saffron from Pampore, which comes in very small sealed plastic containers

- Indian clothing. My favorite store, Fabindia, is found in most Indian cities, and has beautiful clothes for men and women, all at reasonable prices. They also have shops in major airports, where you can browse while waiting for your flight.

If you bring a half empty suitcase you can then fill it with beautiful often inexpensive Indian clothes. Also any clothing you bring can be copied quickly by a local tailor. And most tailor shops also sell a good selection of beautiful fabrics, most often made of good quality cotton.

The art of bargaining

Knowing where and how to bargain for better prices or better quality items is an art well worth developing, if you haven't mastered it already. Not only is bargaining a skill, but shopkeepers often consider it a game—one that, as part of their traditional culture, they seem to enjoy. Don't disappoint them!

Bargaining isn't done in supermarkets, smaller grocery stores, department stores, stores called *emporia* which are often run by the Indian government, most chain stores and many food stalls. Yet even when "fixed price" signs appear, sometimes prominently, in other shops, don't let the sign deter you from asking for a better price. You have nothing to lose.

As in much of the world, foreigners in India often pay double, even triple, what Indians pay. While you may never snap up the Indian price, you can better your chances and up your game by simply using these tried-and-true techniques:

1) Try to be the first customer of the day, as shopkeepers often believe that an early in the day sale means that they'll have a successful sales day. As a result, the first customer may be offered prices that are better than what customers are offered later that same day.

2) Decide what you want to buy, look at prices in a number of other shops, and write them down.

3) Be certain that you're willing to commit to buying an item before starting to bargain. If the shopkeeper ends up agreeing to the price you offer, it's then considered very bad form not to buy it.

4) Decide on the price you're willing to pay, based either on what you've seen elsewhere or just the value of the item to you personally. There isn't any set formula, or percentage, that you should offer.

5) If the price you're offered seems unusually high, a polite playful laugh or chuckle or saying, "Very funny," with a friendly smile, is a good way to start.

6) State your price or ask for a specific discount (e.g. 50%). This amount must be lower than the amount you'll actually accept paying. I often initially offer 40-50% of the price the merchant proposes.

7) If that fails, show the merchant the prices you've written down that were offered by competitors, if you thought those were good.

8) If you see any imperfections in your chosen item, point those out to the merchant.

9) Always look as if you're not really that interested in the item, that you could take it or leave it. A facial expression of bored indifference is often helpful.

10) If there is a language barrier, use your cell phone calculator to display a number in order to show the merchant the price you're willing to pay.

11) The clincher: Take the amount of cash that you're willing to pay out of your pocket (or discretely out of your money belt) and show it to the merchant. This ups your game. (My batting average when I do this isn't 100%, but it's pretty close to it.)

12) If all else fails, then say, "Thank you" and slowly start walking away. Often the merchant will then agree to your price.

13) If I'm bargaining with someone who appears to be very poor, I take that fact into account and bargain a lot less, as that person surely needs those last rupees more than I do.

14) If you really like an item and fall in love with it, and you're best bargaining skills fail, go ahead and buy it, even if the price seems a bit high but not unreasonable. I've often returned home regretting not having bought something that I really liked. Assuming that I'd find the same thing later in my trip often proved wrong. But rarely have I come home with something I'd bought in India, only to conclude that I shouldn't have purchased it.

Have fun bargaining and good luck!

Dealing with money

Let the banks whose credit cards and/or ATM cards you'll be using know that you'll be traveling to India. If you don't they may decline your attempts to use your cards in India.

Although ATMs are a frequent sight in most Indian cities, they are less commonly found in more remote areas. More importantly, even in cities, many don't work, so it's best to stock up on cash when you find a working one. Many limit each transaction to a low amount, often the equivalent of only $140 U.S., so you may need to make several transactions in order to get the amounts you need. Your bank may also limit the amount you can withdraw each day, so check before leaving home.

I've had the best luck in getting the State Bank of India, Citibank, ICICI bank, HDFC bank and Axis bank to accept my U.S. ATM cards.

It's best to travel with ATM cards from at least two different financial institutions, so you can up your odds of success. While most U.S. banks charge a fee for each foreign ATM transaction, not all do, so call around. I use a Charles

Schwab bank ATM card, which is fee-free, but there are also others.

Before traveling to Kashmir check with your tour company to see if any Kashmiri ATMs are currently working in the areas you'll be going to. If you're flying to a major Indian city before heading to Kashmir, try using that airport's ATMs.

Indian currency, the Indian rupee (INR), is officially a controlled currency, so it's not supposed to be taken into or out of India. Therefore you'll need to wait until you arrive in India to purchase Indian rupees. At the end of your trip, convert any unspent Indian money back into U.S. dollars at your departure airport.

To get the current rupee to U.S. dollar exchange rate, check the currency converter at xe.com. The current rate is 72.9 rupees to a U.S. dollar, and the rate hasn't changed much in recent years.

In 2016 the Bank of India withdrew 500 and 1000 rupee banknotes, making them worthless, so avoid accepting these when someone hands you change. Also never accept torn currency, as no one will take it. There is no longer any black market for money exchange in India, so there's no reason to ever exchange money on the street.

If you're able to get small bills in change, cherish and stock up on them, because they're hard to come by. There's a severe shortage of small bills and coins throughout India.

Credit cards are accepted, sometimes with a small fee, at many upscale restaurants, shops and lodgings, and now also at some mid-range ones, and for many airline and train tickets. When paying by card never let your card out of your sight when the transaction is being processed. This avoids an establishment taking your card into a back room, copying it, then using it to rack up fraudulent charges on your account. I've never had this happen in India, but it never hurts to make this a habit.

How to get around

Although taxis weren't running when I was in Kashmir, some seem to be running now. Ola cabs (www.olacabs.com) is India's version of Uber or Lyft. Ola can be used for local rides and even for inter-city or other longer trips. Install the app on your phone, place your order, and you'll be given the driver's license plate number in advance, so you'll know you're getting into the right vehicle.

When buses are running they run between all the major towns I visited in Kashmir.

The nearest train station to Srinagar is Jammu, 166 miles away and a full day (minimum of 8 hours) bus or car ride. For train information check out **irctc.co.in** or **indianrail.gov.in**.

Srinagar is best accessed by plane. For flight information I've found the Indian companies **cleartrip.com**, **makemytrip.com**, and **yatra.com** the most helpful.

If you're walking, to get around locally I ask for directions from local "tuk-tuk" (motorized rickshaw) drivers, taxi drivers, or shopkeepers. If a taxi or tuk-tuk driver insists on driving you and you still prefer to walk, just tell them that you want the exercise. It seems to work. Sometimes it is necessary to ask more than one person, in order to get a consensus. (This is because Indians sometimes will offer you an answer even if they don't know, in order not to appear rude.)

About the author

Author Suzanne Hogsett is an incurable travel addict who's explored some 115 countries and all 50 states.

She spent eighteen years as a tour leader and local guide, created custom itineraries for international travelers, and taught travel seminars for over twenty years at California colleges and universities on *How to Beat the High Cost of Travel, How to Travel Free, Solo Travel, Packing, Tour Conducting, European Travel* and *How to Set Up a Home-based Travel Business.*

She's the author of *Bargain Travel Handbook* (copyright 2002), *How to Set Up a Home-based Travel Business* (copyright 2001), and audio-guide walking and driving tours *Mid-century Modern Palm Springs California,* and *San Francisco's Telegraph Hill Neighborhood,* available from **www.Tours4Mobile.com.**

An inveterate world traveler, she slept on rope beds on a hotel rooftop in Agra India, just across from the Taj Mahal, so she could see it at first light. She rented a room in a house built into Rothenburg Germany's medieval walls, shared hostel dorms next to Martin Luther's Castle Church, in castles on the Rhine River, and on sailboats in Sweden.

After drinking some good Italian wine, she happily sang "O Sole Mio" from a hotel's top floor balcony overlooking a Venetian canal, and she gazed down upon the glistening Dome of the Rock in Jerusalem from a hotel on the Mount of Olives. She chose rickety tree-house rooms on tea plantations, cave rooms in Turkey's Cappadoccia, and yurt camps in Uzbekistan in Central Asia.

She sought out less frequented sights: London's Old Bailey courthouse, where the attorneys and judges still wear curly white powdered wigs, a mirrored Persian mosque in Damascus Syria, colossal limestone heads of gods at Mt. Nemrut in southeastern Turkey, Buddhist monasteries in Ladakh India, Mao Tse Tung's farmhouse in rural China, the Sunday animal market in Kashgar China, and the Lower East Side Tenement Museum in Manhattan.

In Slovenia she soaked in perhaps the world's biggest hot tub. As a student in Paris she read her French textbooks in a quiet corner of the Notre Dame Cathedral. She stood in awe at the pulpit that Dr. Martin Luther King, Jr. preached from in Montgomery Alabama, and she sat in on pivotal cases in the United States' Supreme Court.

She sat atop the bright red Sossesvlei sand dunes in Namibia, a Mayan pyramid in Palenque Yucatan, Mexico that overlooked a lush jungle, and temples in Pagan Myanmar (Burma), where she could hear the sounds of monks chanting and bicycle bells ringing in the valley below. She walked atop ancient city walls in Khiva Uzbekistan, on a less explored part of the Great Wall of China, and in Rothenburg, on Germany's Romantic Road.

She first saw the special light on the sands and waters of the French Riviera, as she arrived at water's edge still sleepy in an overnight train. She had memorable views of Greek Orthodox Christian monasteries perched atop hilltops in Meteora Greece, and of Samarkand Uzbekistan's remarkable Islamic architecture in its Registan Square. She first saw Mt. Everest from base camp at 18,000 feet in Tibet, and she joyfully crossed the Golden Gate Bridge, as it welcomed her into her new life in San Francisco. She arose early to see Sikkim India's snow-capped Himalayan Mt. Kanchenjunga up close at sunrise, and she climbed 3,000 feet to gaze upon and visit Bhutan's 10,000 feet high Tiger's Nest Monastery, perched high on a mountaintop.

She met special people close to home and in the farthest flung places: the Aboriginals in Australia's red center, the "Blue Men" in Morocco, the Syrians who yelled, "We love Americans," the Kurds in Eastern Turkey who invited her to dinner, the Muslim fishermen in a small village in Southern India, the traditional hill villagers of Sapa North Vietnam, the farmers in the Bolivian highlands, and those in Iowa's flatlands. She sang hymns with thousands of others in a Brooklyn Tabernacle, realized that what she thought were women were really men on Bugis Street in Singapore in its heyday, and she witnessed up close the resilience and fortitude of the victims of the 2015 earthquake in Kathmandu Nepal.

She loved to immerse herself in nature, far from "civilization," where white rhinos crossed just in front of her Landrover in Assam India and in South Africa's Kruger National Park, where lions rested on the road at night in Tanzania, where majestic tigers could be seen up close in India's

Ranthambore National Park, and orangutans swayed from trees in Sumatra. On Sundays in West Africa's Côte d'Ivoire (Ivory Coast) she hitched rides on a small private plane and flew at fifty feet, just above magnificent herds of elephants. But perhaps her best experience in nature was in western Thailand, where she swam with elephants and bathed them in a river.

She found the Muslim call to prayer from a Turkish mosque's minaret mesmerizing on day one, but by day three she complained when it woke her up out of a sound sleep at 5 a.m. She heard Dixieland jazz on the streets of New Orleans, and sang Mexican folk songs accompanied by a local Indian guitarist in a lantern-lit garden on the edge of Mexico's Copper Canyon. Adorned with marigolds and barefoot, she chanted to drumbeats in Amritsar India's Sikh Golden Temple, and to others along India's sacred Ganges River at Rishikesh.

She tried fatty camel meat under the stars at a Bedouin camp in the Jordanian desert, and ate kebabs behind a restaurant curtain in Afghanistan, as women diners were separated from the men. She caught large wild salmon in Alaska and Dungeness crab off a pier on the Oregon coast. She learned that Singaporean chili crab was best eaten only with her hands and that the tasteless mushrooms on her pizza in Bali turned out to be hallucinogenic. (Did that explain why, just after eating it, she ventured out into the Indian Ocean and thought that she was a mermaid?) She enjoyed sitting cross-legged on the floor with some one thousand other diners, eating dal and rice in a Sikh temple's "poor kitchen" in India.

She found that flying at times was uncertain at best. On a flight in the Himalayas a pounding lightning and hail storm shook her plane violently for hours and threatened to down it. She was taken off a plane in Myanmar (Burma) at gunpoint when some soldiers wanted her seat and she didn't want to give it up, and a flight on Bhutan's Drukair into Paro's mountainous airspace required a "dive landing." Her most jarring airline incident was a terrorist attempt on her flight, when they threatened to hijack and crash her plane. (Fortunately the U.S. State Department foiled the plot at the last minute.)

She crossed southern Africa's Kalahari desert in a rental car, zooming over hills and dips and slippery turns, as she used the rental company's list of "don't drive tos" as a splendid itinerary. She reached the world's highest navigable road in Ladakh India at 19,300 feet, and traveled with a Buddhist monk in an open-air Landrover from New Delhi to Tehran, going through the Khyber Pass.

She loved her journeys by train—the two-day ride from western China's Xining that chugged up, up, up to Lhasa Tibet, and a rail trip to see China's ancient Silk Road treasure cities of Jiayuguan, Dunhuang, Turpan, Urumchi and Kashgar. On Rovos Rail from Capetown to Pretoria South Africa she bathed in a Victorian era bathtub, where she watched wildlife roaming just outside her window. On the Trans-Australian railway she viewed "big red" kangaroos, and she spent many months in India perched on top bunks on slower than slow trains, just watching India roll, and sometimes crawl, by.

She biked along the Danube River's Wine Route in Austria, atop Lucca Italy's ancient wall, on narrow paths leading through rice paddies among karst mountain landscapes in Yangshuo China, and she searched for big crabs while biking around then undiscovered Huahine Island in Tahiti.

She saw the Taj Mahal at full moon, with no other lighting, in a bicycle rickshaw, and roamed Beijing's narrow residential alleyways (hutongs). She crossed Egypt's Suez Canal in a local bus, accompanied by armed guards, and boarded a packed local bus which sped through Beijing's outlying villages, in search of the best Peking duck restaurant. And, of course, she looks forward to more adventures to come.

Suzanne lives in Palm Springs, California with her husband and Persian cat.

She can be reached at **suzannehogsett@gmail.com**.
Also visit her website **suzannetravels.com**.
(It includes many color photos.)

A note from the author

I'd love to hear from you

I enjoy hearing from all of my readers, so please feel free to e-mail me with any comments. If you liked this book, a review of any length would be greatly appreciated. If you've bought this book from Amazon, just go to **amazon.com,** find this title, click on ratings, and write what you think. Or, you can just e-mail me a review if you'd prefer.

Happy Travels!
Suzanne

www.ingramcontent.com/pod-product-compliance
Lightning Source LLC
Chambersburg PA
CBHW071526080526
44588CB00011B/1564